THE STUD'S GUIDE FOR BUYING FLOWERS

….give those bouquets, get yourself laid!

By Joe Guggia AIFD

I0163115

So Why The Hell Do I Need To Read This Thing?

I have a news flash for all you studs that is going to change your life and make me the most awesome guy you know: buying flowers for your wife, partner, mistress, lover or whomever you're sleeping with is the best thing you can do for your sex life and all around well-being. While you might be one of those guys that wants to blurt out "but flowers are expensive!" stop that crap right this second and listen to what I have to say. Trust me that by spending a few bucks here and there on flowers, you can become a wanted lover that will turn your sometimes boring sex life into the romantically overheated experience you want and need. Know that giving beautiful flowers is an asset to your daily life that will make all your relationships (family, friends, lovers, fellow workers) respond in a positive way to your being.

This world is definitely full of constant surprises and it changes at a moment's notice. Everyday we're confronted with something new that grabs our balls and tests us to the max. We get up and go about life hoping that at least one thing we do really makes a difference in our world and the world of those around us. But sometimes there are those crappy things that get the best of us and we just want to run a hundred miles an hour and yell "screw you!" at the top of our lungs.

We feel that way sometimes, friggn' overwhelmed and just plain tired of all the crap that's thrown our way. So buying flowers should be one of those experiences we can handle easily and not be confused about. It's the kind of experience you should want to do over and over again so you can give that someone special in your life a great gift that they'll love you up for. With proper flower buying knowledge you can learn to give something beautiful and get back what you're hoping for tenfold. This fact has been proven over and over again, has gone on for centuries and will continue to go on for centuries more. Humans are created that way, responding in an incredibly positive way to receiving nature's gift of flowers for any and every occasion.

So trust me and take a few minutes away from that game, food, garage or whatever the hell has your attention. Read and absorb what I have to say. Follow the techniques I explain in this flower buying bible and be ready to learn how the simplest of bouquets will show them how hot you think they are. This floral education is sure to get your special someone right where you want them to be, ready and willing to reward you with the best "thank you" you could ever imagine. And if you were only reading this because someone threw it in front of you and said "Honey, read this!" don't give them any flack and just do it. This will be the one time you'll be damn glad you did!

Monkey Men Had It Goin' On

You might not think it, but this history lesson is very important for the flower buying journey that we're traveling on. Finding out that this custom dates back to prehistoric times lets us know that giving flowers must get results for those monkey faced guys to have done it. Read on to understand how flowers have played such an important part in the world for centuries.

Giving and using flowers dates back to prehistoric times when cave men used flowers for taking care of medicinal needs, grinding and heating their blooms and leaves for different physical ailments. Early Romans, Greeks, Egyptians, and Chinese used flowers to show their emotions and get their lover in the sack just as you should do today. This is when Greek and Roman mythology started the custom of using that cutey Cupid (the son of Venus, goddess of love) as the symbol for the celebration of love and lovers. The custom of giving flowers kept going on through to the middle ages, with France and England playing important roles in this custom of flower giving. The churches during that time wouldn't let you show open affection in public (no, not even a sneaky pat on the butt) so everyone let flowers do the talking.

This was also a time when flowers became popular as gifts for theater groups using a bouquet placed on stage as bad luck but giving that bouquet at the end of the performance to a leading lady meant good luck (go studs!). And Get this: in the 1700s, Sweden used flowers during war time to send messages back and forth, with the other team thinking they were just getting a gift! The subtle yet romantic Victorians started the custom of giving red roses to their lady, but if you sent them upside down, lookout, that was meant to piss her off. Guess that might work sometimes, but I think we're trying to go a different direction, right?

The custom of giving flowers has been carried on to the present and is practiced all over the world. Most television shows and movies have bouquets setting on tables, being given and enjoyed by viewers and staff. Talk shows are especially in tune to the beauty of flowers as well with bouquets around their conversation areas. There are all kinds of customs associated with flower giving and it's obvious that centuries have proven that the practice of giving flowers brings happiness over and over again. This bit of history should give you disbelievers a little more confidence that this system really works. Flower giving is a "profitable" exercise to practice your whole life, with great rewards close at hand.

The Village Of Testosterone

There's one thing I know to be darn true in this world: we men are definitely testosterone driven beings! It's a great thing we're blessed with, but also need to understand if we're going to have successful lives. Channel it the right way, and a hell of a lot can be achieved. Go down another path and a lot of crap can be brought into your life. Understanding that testosterone plays a huge roll in your life is key to a fulfilling and prosperous (sexually and otherwise) life.

Let me point out a few things that are ruled by this awesome sex spice:

Survival of our genetic pool —

Okay people, we know that besides food, water, and air, sex is the main driving force for most of our actions in this world. We constantly want to attract that other person to make them feel comfortable and safe, so we can ultimately have an orgasm and show our true machismo. Testosterone levels maintain this motivation and we want those levels to stay as high as possible allowing our best performance at all times. This fact is proven daily by the pharmaceutical industry that has created a whole bunch of goodies that keep us "at attention" for hours at a time showing how important this is in our lives.

Bringing home the butter —

This is one place where we better have HUGE balls to show off our macho stuff. I mean, come on, we've got mouths to feed, bosses to impress, and golf buddies that need to think we're hot shit. Tons of competition out there that need proof we can perform better than them. If those weak pussies are in the way, watch out 'cause we're gonna run 'em over and prove that we've got that hormone ten times more than they do!

The sports phenomena--

Let's be real: anybody worth their anything is a big sports guy. We want to be them, play like them, be their best friend, and make all that money doing something that seems so incredibly natural and fun. And that driving force for all of these guys is, yup that wonderful hormone testosterone. Without it, there would be no sports world, no boxing, football, baseball, basketball, soccer, golf, any of it. No big money for all our youngsters to yearn for. No parents on the sideline cheering for their kid that they know MUST be the best on that field or court.

You're probably thinking "Yeah, and what's this idiot trying to say about buying flowers with all this testosterone crap?!". Here's the deal: testosterone makes you want sex, and you can't always just have it (well, I know there are quickie ways, but I can't take care of everything for you) so you need my professional guidance to get you there. That's where the proper information for flower buying will really bring it all home (or wherever you guys end up). The next chapters will explain it all, helping you get the results you're looking for while spending the right amount of bucks for the best value and fun experience. Even one simple flower makes the sentiment go a long way. Get this practice of sending flowers going and keep it up (pun intended) till your 80 plus to continue a fun and rewarding sex life. You'll be the one that they're glad they hooked up with, ready to fulfill their wildest dreams, keeping you and them happy and productive in life.

The New Hottie And The Village Screamers

Shit, are new relationships a macho test or what?! Especially when our testosterone level has shot way up there and we want to get it all going. You meet someone at a bar or wedding, the attraction is immediate and you want the journey to get going. A couple phone calls later a date is set up.

Now you don't want to scare the newbie off, but you think it would be a good idea to send or bring flowers. Here's where the floral expertise comes into play. The best choice in this case is to have a wrapped bouquet of one variety of white flowers, like tulips or orchids, and 6 or 12 stems is a fine amount to use. This is very sophisticated and will let them know that you have style and class. You may be the most ill-mannered S.O.B. there is but you want this hottie to think you're the coolest man around, and to convince them you know your shit. It's best if you pre-order this at your florist so it can be created and ready for you. Don't have it be all baby breathed up, either. The flowers with touches of greenery are the way to go, and the simplicity of this bouquet will send the right message that you're a styln' dude.

I'm sure success on this first date will be due to my floral suggestions, although your charm and debonair attitude may have played SOME part. If you got them in the sack, awesome job! If not, you'll keep the game going. In any case, if the date went well, an arrangement of some sort should be delivered to their work the next week. This is when the smaller vase designs are the ticket. You don't want to lam blast them with this big 'ol floral thing saying "I dig you so much I want to spend the rest of my life with you!". That will scare the crap out of them for sure! Just something subtle and beautiful that shows your appreciation and your classy style. A larger version of the loose flowers you gave on the first date is a killer idea: same flowers in an arranged bouquet to show what an awesome time you had and that you're looking forward to more. More what, time will tell. After this point you need to see how things progress and you'll have a better understanding where the relationship is heading. You know by now that flowers will continue to play an important role in this romantic story so make sure to use them to your best advantage.

In-House Tail Maintenance

Well, looks like all those dating flowers did the trick, 'cause now you're married or cohabitating with the current love of your life. You probably thought you were free and clear of the flower buying, but you are dead wrong dude. You have many more required years of spreading floral beauty in order to keep receiving your sexual gifts.

For many guys Valentine's Day, anniversary, and birthday flower buying have been pretty much embedded in their head after being in a relationship. These holidays usually are a given by then and the pattern has been set and receiving flowers will be expected, which is just part of the deal. With some experience you have come to understand what your person likes (and definitely what they don't like!) and this should be a smooth sailing venture. You'll know if they love roses, hate carnations, or really don't give a crap what kind they get as long as you send flowers. And if you haven't paid attention like most of us dumb asses, please start. It's never too late to surprise someone with your knowledge of their being, and knowing what flowers they like is a great asset to your relationship. Show that you still care with a little extra thoughtfulness that really keeps the romance alive. If you just aren't sure what the person likes, it's still ok and you're forgiven. Florists create lots of orders that are "designer's choice" making flower arrangements that wow them with each order (kind of a test, which we designers all love). Once this is proven to you, and the recipient is pleased, it makes everyone's life much easier. You can just say "send beautiful flowers for my anniversary" and we do our job. It's a safe bet that you will be well appreciated for your efforts, with a physical "thank you" right around the corner. The florist again becomes your best ally in the ongoing world of relationships.

Now, special birthday and anniversary years deserve a little more attention. Larger bouquets are usually sent for 5 year increments: 5th anniversary, 25th birthday, etc. Dig a little deeper into those pockets so you can really "wow" them with some special attention and make the office staff jealous as well. By the way, I can't tell you how much it pleases people to receive flowers at work. It's gotta be the all-time best place to get that arrangement. And always sign them with your name. Some guys say "oh, they'll know who they're from" and guess what, sometimes they don't! I've had occasions where there was some funny stuff going on at that workplace and, because there was no signature, the spouse thought it was from the guy in the other office. Man, did that cause some friction in their relationship!

It won't hurt you every now and then to just come home with some flowers. They can be just a few stems wrapped together, or just one simple flower works. This special thought is incredible for a great roll in the hay, and just relationship well-being. Try to mark your work calendar or computer calendar 1 day a month to do this. Yeah, we're all busy, but this is really important especially when all our lives are so hectic. Get used to stopping by your favorite florist to pick up those posies and make sure you carry the plan through. Once you get used to the habit (and your lover does) it will be an ongoing custom that is sure to PLEASE.

Flowers vs. Plants: Testes On The Cutting Block

Once you've lived with your significant other for some years, chances are (and I'm sure they have let you know!) you will have a clue as to what they like in this gift category. There are going to be many partners that have extreme fiscal responsibility and their practicality is definitely at the fore front: flowers to them are just a plain waste of your family's hard earned money. They are sure to yell "Don't buy me flowers, they just die! Give me a plant that lasts!". I have news for these people that EVERYTHING is going to die, so buck up and smell the roses. This realization will be embedded in your head forever and if you were to come home with fresh cut flowers your head and/or genitals could be placed on that mini guillotine that is stashed in the closet.

By this time in your relationship you'd be smart to have picked up on the type of fresh plants that your loved one likes by hearing key words such as "hydrangea", "violet", "orchid", "tropical". Having this knowledge can really make your life easier and please your loved one. If you don't have a clue to the variety of plant you should get, my suggestion is to always get something blooming. That way it has beautiful color and will give you more points than just a plain green plant. One Valentine's Day a young man came into our flower shop looking for a plant for his new wife. He was standing next to a large leafed philodendron (old school looking for sure) feeling the foliage and viewing the whole plant. Asking if I could help him he replied "I'm looking for something for my new wife. She's really hot, and told me she loves plants. This one's so nice and big; I really think she'll like it!" meaning "the bigger it is, the more she'll think I love her, and the more kind of sex I want I'll get!". Knowing this just ain't the kind of plant his pretty young thing would want, I steered him towards a beautiful section of orchids, explaining how the simple sophistication and beauty of these plants would represent the "hotness" of his wife much better than that philodendron. I got a call the next week thanking me for my help, referring to the fact that the gift REALLY made his wife happy. Another pleasure seeker getting what he wanted by bringing home the right floral gift!

So listen to what they have to say (make your life MUCH easier and always listen) and get an idea of what your hottie likes in the plant world. If it's outdoor plants, then learn what the yard needs and buy accordingly. Yes, you'll probably be the one who has to plant the things, but don't bitch about it and learn that it's just the finishing touch of the complete gift. If you have no clue as to the plant choice you should give, definitely give the florist an idea of the style or colors they like which will help define the choice. Using terms like "French country" "contemporary" "natural" are nice clues for the sales person as to the type of foliage to be purchased. Then the florist can decorate the plant to enhance the lifestyle of the person, making it a much more special gift. Hate to bring it up again (oh sure!) but my wonderful years of floral experience have again assisted you with your continuing romantic roll-in-the-hay journey. You've learned to purchase an everyday gift and turn it into that most memorable of experiences that will be well rewarded.

Sexy Roses Of A Different Color

For years sending red roses has been thought of as the best expression of love. It's been something ingrained in our brains, and most are convinced that sending red roses will get them great sex. In many cases, sending these beautiful flowers is what's expected and should be done. And in just as many cases the person receiving these flowers is afraid to let that stud know they'd rather receive another color. I've learned over the last few years that most people really don't like red roses as much as they used to. I'm sure that will change by generation and something the floral world needs to be aware of. Recently we've found that most are in love with the other beautiful colors that are available: mixed pinks, faded yellows, vibrant peaches/oranges, subtle lavenders, creamy whites. With so many new varieties of roses grown every year, the color choices are incredible. There are great shades of all colors that friends and partners would love to receive and their favorites are sure to be in these selections. Don't be a chicken shit, try these different rose colors. Hopefully you're aware of their color likes, but if you're like most of us, it goes in one ear and out the other. If that's the case, take a chance and send one of these different colors showing that you are today's modern guy who knows his macho stuff. Rely on your florist for this info if you're not sure. If they love the color the person receives, play it off as if it was totally your idea. If not, blame it on the florist! Trust me, we're used to it and we can take it. But 99% of the time we're right so you can trust our great floral knowledge.

If nothing else, using roses in an arrangement of mixed flowers will definitely give you many points on the plus side of the scoreboard of love. Roses have always been perceived as an upscale flower with great value, just as orchids and tropical varieties are. This *perceived value* is an incredible asset in the point system of love. Just as the bigger the diamond shows the more you love them, the more quality the floral arrangement you give convinces them just how much you care. Here we have another occasion where handling the floral experience in a positive way will net you that wonderful boner bonus. Wow, who'd have thought it could be so much fun giving damn flowers!

Mommy And Family Need Lovn' Too!

While hot sex flowers are very important, you can't forget family that's been in your life and helped you through all those crappy times when you really screwed up. Of course, the most important person to remember is your mommy. She nurtured you, listened to you, gave you money when you needed it, and did things that no person ever has or will for you (like wiping your butt!). These flowers just need to be beautiful and she'll love whatever you send her, unless she's one of those bitchy ones that says "He knows I don't like red!" and, trust me, they do exist. If your mom is like that, then make sure you know what she doesn't like. That will save your ears from the ringing you remember when you got bitched at as a child. Flower arrangements for moms are best designed with a mixture of flowers and colors. These really say that you're thinking about her and love her. Well worth a thousand points in the mother/child world of pluses and minuses. And it's the safest type of flower arrangement to send. If you know the color she loves, fine, send an arrangement of all one color. But if you're like most of us you don't have a clue what flowers she likes so rely on your florist again to direct you to the proper arrangement.

Sometimes an arrangement in a "keepsake" container (like a nice quality ceramic vase that can be used as a décor accessory) is the key versus a cheap basket or glass vase. That container gives a more valuable impression and has residual value for later use. There are lots of these container options to choose from, and she will have something of quality left after the flowers have done their thing. And if she's one of those thrifty moms, she'll love that her little boy used his head and spent money on something of lasting value as well as beautiful flowers.

This is also a case where plants are a great option. I'm sure she has some straggly piece-of-crap plant in the house that she's kept barely alive for the last decade because it came from Uncle Leo's funeral. Even though she'll probably keep the funky one, a new plant will at least make you feel better when you go to her house. Something durable with nice decorations (willow, ribbons, maybe a bird or two, they seem to love that) is a great plant choice, and your friendly florist will help you make the proper selection. The blooming plant is also a safe bet here too. Something that can be planted outside in the yard after a bit is a good choice for maternal longevity. She can gaze out at the yard and remember her dear little boy who still loves her. Or at least remembered her frigging birthday for a change!

Flower buying for a sibling is also a special way to show you're a caring SOB. Yeah, you guys probably beat the crap out of each other, or you locked them in a closet (unless you got locked in) for a few hours listening to the screaming, whining and pissing on the floor. But the fact is, you really do love them and want to acknowledge their achievements. There are so many occasions in life where the gift of flowers really makes the event special: their job promotions, a great tit job, arrival of a new baby, an engagement, they got out of jail, finally got the divorce, the much awaited penile enlargement. The list goes on. It doesn't matter if they're a guy or a girl, it's always appreciated to receive a gift, and flowers are the easiest thing to send that makes the most impression. A cool office plant creation is a great way to celebrate with them, as well as a creative, artsy fresh design. The sky's the limit, and you're the captain of this ship. Don't forget the residual value I keep mentioning. In this case it's family comradery and we all know that can be an incredible asset in our lives, especially when we need money or to get bailed out of jail.

This information also applies to aunts/uncles, godmothers/godfathers, grandmothers/grandfathers. Grandmothers are the real special ones to remember because they've usually played an important role in most of our lives. My parents were always at my kid's sports games, graduations, pre-prom photos and anything else that had to do with their celebrations or changes in life. Their time seems to be more available and the fact that their heritage is continuing really excites their being. That generation seems to love receiving flowers and they think it's just so "cute" when their grandchild sends them. For some reason the respect of a grandchild is so important and is truly reinforced when a gift is received by them (and a place in the will doesn't hurt either!)

For grandmothers, the sweeter the better. Little mixed nosegays in a vase do the trick, as well as tea cups with little roses. And I don't think this will change with the next generation. Don't get me wrong, there are plenty of hip grandmas out there that love cool designs with architectural interest. The way their houses are decorated and the way they dress will tune you in to that fact. Some of these grandmas were hippies in the '60s and '70s and probably still smoke a little bit of cannabis through their day to keep that "peace and love" still traveling. And they're sure to dig a creative floral design or plant and think it's *groovay*.

Don't think because the grandfather is from the generation where flowers are thought to be just for woman that they don't like to receive them. But here's where they really like to get a container that represents their life. The golfers love those containers with a golf theme, or the fisherman who receives tackle paraphernalia in his design. They'll think it's just as damn cute as that little tea cup. This is where your gifted florist truly comes in handy. Their job is to come up with these creative additions to make that design really special. And they should also be willing to get their butts out there and purchase the items you want to make that arrangement special for you. That's the mark of a true artist and professional friend, where forming a great relationship with your florist is a continued asset.

The Neighborhood Piss Off

The fact is, there are just times in our lives when we screw up. Maybe the intention wasn't there, but we sure as hell end up pissing someone off. Take, for example, the innocent celebration of a promotion, or a cocktail party we have for a few college friends who happen to be in town. The event starts out cool and calm, but as the evening wears on, those martinis and brewskies just keep piling up and making our group PARTEEEE! Then starts the rockn' music, with Freddy Mercury at the helm getting us all goin', dancing, and singing with those crappy loud voices that are so aggravating to the outside world. And, of course, the windows and doors HAVE to be thrown open 'cause the sweat just keeps rolling off with all that gyratn' and sleezy dancn'. That's when those wonderful sounds float through the neighborhood, serenading man and beast with earfuls that would piss anybody off at 3am. There's also those times your damn beagle hears sirens and howls for hours. If you've ever had that breed, you know there ain't nothin' gonna stop that howling. You can chase, beat, crush, yell and threaten with just about anything, and the animal just won't stop.

So after all these things settle down, the choice of flowers for the neighborhood or apartment complex is just the ticket. I don't mean to say that you have to spend a fortune on larger arrangements for each neighbor. I'm talking about a single stemmed flower (such as a sunflower or gerbera daisy, those "happy" looking flowers) wrapped nicely in cellophane or some sort of paper tied with a ribbon. Attach a hand written note (signed by you so it's more personal) that says something like "Please accept my apology for our loud celebration last night. We were just so excited about my promotion!" Letting them know you got a promotion or had something special happen in your life will make them feel less angry and maybe even happy for you. Just leave the flowers near their front door like a quiet little leprechaun who stole away in the night, even if your head is pounding and you want to puke your guts out at each doorway. So whether it's the dog, office celebration, cutting the tree too far over on their side (a biggy 'cause they really had a fondness for that tree), chasing tail in the neighborhood, or yelling "screw you asshole!" to the guy that drives too fast into his driveway, make amends by giving simple flowers. We've done that for years in our neighborhoods (although we're not complete dumb asses all the time) and the gesture is really appreciated. Better yet, invite them over the next time so they can share in the great news you've just gotten. And who knows, you might get lucky and that neighbor tail might just invite over that other neighbor tail for the three way you've been thinkn' about for years!

Kiss Some Corporate Ass!

We all work hard every day and really want our work relationships to go well. If we get along with our fellow workers, the day goes by in a much more pleasant way. We do lunches together, go out for drinks after work, and spend some special occasions together. But sometimes your work friends might have some personal stress going on in their lives that warrants a little happy "boost" that flowers can give. Or a good job they did on some project. I'm just talking about a small vase with a single flower or a mixture of flowers that your florist puts together. Maybe a small container of plants or an orchid that would fit on their desk. Nothing elaborate, just a nice, thoughtful gesture.

Now, you're going to have to be the judge of how this goes. If it's someone whose pants you want to get into, that's another story and you need to follow the previous instructions I've given. But this is a chance to make someone's day so much better, letting them know they are important in your life and that you care. This works well for a group of you to go in together on the floral gift. Birthdays, special work anniversaries, promotions, etc. are great occasions to send flowers. This goes for management as well (which really can add points in the plus column). With today's technology and social networking, it's easy to find out someone's birthday if you don't already know. And coming from a group is so appreciated and makes the recipient feel pretty darn special.

Think about this and start getting it into action. Receiving flowers in an office or work atmosphere is one of the best things that can happen. It just gets the group excited and really is an asset to enjoying that special day for everyone.

Hasta La Vista, Baby!

Buying and sending flowers when someone dies is a very scary thought to most guys. We're all aware it's going to happen, but when it's reality, we just don't quite know what to do. Sending flowers has been a custom to say you're sorry for that kickn' for many years, and still is the best and easiest thing you can do to let the family know that you're thinking of them.

The great thing is if you don't want to see the family in person, or just hate the total funeral agenda (which ain't no fun if you ask me), you can simply pick up the phone and call your favorite florist and they can do the job for you without any personal involvement whatsoever. A nice safety net to enjoy, and life doesn't provide a whole lot of these. Why go through all that drama when it's totally unnecessary? Your florist can select the proper item to send to the service, or you can send a great floral design or plant to the home for them to enjoy. It truly is that simple. But I know some of you studs are still going to go into the flower shop in person, look through the catalogue, and make your own selection, or at least try to be in control of the situation. So be it. But just put as much of it in the hands of the floral designers so they can create something special that will represent you well. My years of experience tell me that traditional funeral arrangements are a thing of the past. By traditional I mean one of those triangular jobs of funky flowers like carnations or mums with no creative design. It's much cooler to send something that has style and will make the recipients feel better than some old funeral looking thing. Let the shop be creative and do a wonderful job for you. Now if it's a close family member, then it's going to be a different story. In this case the flowers are going to need to really represent what that person was in their life, whether it be a gardener, prostitute, hunter, philanderer, thief, fisherman, or whatever. You'll probably have to think a bit on this because most people aren't immediately aware of the bucket kicker's favorite color or style. The shop can also add items to the sympathy designs (that you'll get back, of course) to make the flowers really pop. I've added fishing poles, golf clubs, boots, flower pots, and many other items to make the designs special for the family or friends. Whatever you bring in, the designers can add. Don't be afraid of all this funeral stuff. It's just part of the game of life and in my mind should be a wonderful celebration of someone's journey instead of a drab, tearfully sad occasion. And please, don't wear black to the funeral. It drives me crazy! It's so much nicer to see some beautifully colored outfits that depict a great life and adds a much more uplifting atmosphere to the occasion.

It's A Brave New World: The Cyber Florist Seduction

Now that I've got your relationship flowers defined for all you studs, I need to direct you in the proper way to actually *buy* the flowers. We all know that the internet is the best place to research anything our brain can think of. It's an incredible entity where our manly fingers can simply stroke those keys to give us what our hearts desire. But when it comes to flower buying, I'm not so sure the Cyber Florist is the best place for guys to go. On the Net there are tons of "store front" sites that show you all kinds of floral pictures. You pick out something you think your person will like, and they end up sending the order to a flower shop that might be right around the corner from you. I'll admit it's quick, easy and a no brainer way to order flowers. But in reality, many of these cyber stores are just order taking places that charge you an extra fee (some add on $14.99) for doing this small job of sending the order to a brick and mortar flower shop. My goal is to show you how to search and find a *real* florist that can be a true asset to your relationships. Now, if you don't care about service and quality, then don't waste your precious time on this chapter. I know you've got a very important life to take care of, and time is a valuable asset. But if you want to receive those great sexual and life rewards that flower giving can bring you, let me mouth off some more about this great floral knowledge that I've got.

These "order gathering" middle men receive a percentage (usually 20%) for just being order takers plus that extra dollar amount for the service. They have a site with all kinds of generic images that can be viewed by people like you who may not have a clue what to order, can just click on a floral something, give their information and be done with it. Then these middle men simply pass the flower order on to a retail flower shop that gets only about 73% of the dollar amount you've spent and are expected to design the arrangement at 100% value. Now I'm no genius, but I sure as hell want to get 100% of the money for the value I'm giving to my client. There's a variety of these order takers, but the most popular seem to be 1-800-Flowers.com, Just Flowers.com, Blooms Today.com, From You Flowers.com, FTD.com, Teleflora.com., and more. It's not an awful thing to order from these vendors, but going directly through your local florist is a much better value for everyone, and will save you money on those service charges.

Many of these internet middlemen outsource their orders to operators that are thousands of miles away in other countries. Trust me, this ain't a good thing. All the person does is look at the flower picture, hit a few keys on the keyboard with your information, and pass it on to a real florist who designs the arrangement and delivers it. No creative wheels turning there. If you have detailed questions, they generally can't give you the answer you need. I've taken orders from some of these people, and their skills really need some fine tuning. It scares me a bit that so many flower buyers are using them because they think it's the only way to buy flowers.

If you want to order flowers using the internet as a resource, search for a real flower shop (meaning a florist that has a physical store and location) that will have a true professional answering the phone. Searching for a brick and mortar shop in your area should be simple and not a bit stressful. On your computer use the search terms "flower shops in (your city)" and while a bunch of the middle men will pop up, take a minute to scroll the list and check for listings that will direct you to a real flower shop's website. Click on the site address and check out their web site. Click on the "about us" section so you can read about the owners, experience, how long in the area, etc. This will give you a good indication about the job they will do. From the flower arrangement images get an idea of the type of arrangement you'd like to send. Then call them and discuss this with the florist so you can feel confident with their work. Florists can use the images as a guideline, but also like to let the client know that they can adjust these designs to give a custom and creative edge to the design. As a side note, a problem that does occur is that buyers think everything should look like the picture. It's tough for florists to always carry the total inventory necessary, or the florist can run out of the product listed. That's why the personal connection is much better to discuss alternate options. You might think "Hey, if the pictures are there shouldn't they have those flowers?". But fresh flowers aren't like shoes that can be manufactured and stored for lengths of time, nor should they be. They're a fresh item that needs to be bought daily (good thing for you guys) to maintain freshness and quality, and sometimes the inventory gets depleted before we know it. So be aware of this fact, and give a little slack for the creative mind to work for your benefit.

After a few minutes of conversation you'll feel comfortable with your choice and you'll know that you can let them do their job. You can also feel very secure that if you do your order strictly on line with the flower shop's web site that it will be carried out in a professional way. I cannot impress to you how much better for our economy that working directly with a flower shop is. It really helps the locally owned retail flower shops increase their volume, while giving you the personal service that is really important in today's world.

So here's the deal: use the internet for your flower shop research, establish a relationship with the chosen shop, and let them do their job. They will deliver incredible bouquets to that someone special for you, and I know you'll be glad you took the extra time to do that research.

Once you've researched and decided on the flower shop you'd like to use, you might want to go there in person to see their choices and place your order in person. Some of you might have a little apprehension of this "unknown", but if you come in with the right attitude and let everyone do their job, it will be a wonderful experience. Some of you might want to go there and be in control but just can't because of the lack of floral knowledge. Some of you will walk in and spin your heads around trying to see something familiar that you can focus on. Others will come in with extreme machismo and the "I'm here to take care of my lover babe" attitude. While I get how you feel, it's just not necessary and you need to cool your balls and get rid of that feeling of intimidation. No one's trying to scare you, rip you off or control your life. It's really important for this experience to be positive so that your future flower buying can run efficiently, with each trip to the flower shop being easier and more positive.

You also don't need to think that you have to look at endless pictures in a book that will confuse the hell out of you more than help you. Just walk in calmly viewing the showroom and checking it all out. This will be a great experience, especially if you allow everyone to do their job. Be sure to tell the sales person or greeter how awesome the shop looks. This will really make them feel great and they'll become your best friend. Florists love compliments (don't we all!) so learn to play on that fact and it will take you a long way with better value and service. Trust me, compliments are a wonderful thing to give, and they are absolutely free. It's also a plus if you come in with a great attitude. Some guys come in the shop acting like "I gotta do this, 'cause if I don't, I'm in big trouble!" We all understand where you're coming from, but get that shitty attitude out of your head. Come in, enjoy it, and feel good about it.

One important thing for your comfort is to have all the relevant information for the flower delivery you want to send. Some guys will give an address, but not say that it's a business. Or they won't have a phone number. Or sometimes not even a first or last name (believe it!). While florists are great information researchers, their time is much better spent on creating a beautiful arrangement of flowers for you.

Here's the information that's really important for you to give the florist:

1. The full name of who the flowers are going to (yes, first AND last name are a must, especially for delivery purposes).

2. You'll need to know where you want the flowers sent, whether it's to the home or business.

3. Have the address of the home or business plus the business name (that really helps the delivery person so they can look for signage, etc.).

4. Give the phone numbers for the delivery location and the cell number for the recipient. Many deliveries I've made would have been much simpler if I've had a cell number to immediately connect with the recipient in case they aren't at the expected delivery location. Also, *please* let them also know if there are any specific times the recipient leaves or won't be at the location. This is extremely helpful.

5. If you have an idea of the type of flowers or color they love or hate, be sure to add that info into the equation (a good florist should ask those questions anyway).

Here's some sample dialogue to give you an idea how the order should go. Each order has different qualities, but this shows how a competent sales staff member should handle the order.

Florist: "Hi, how are you and how may I help you today?"

You: "I'm great and looking for a floral gift for my wife."

Florist: "That's so nice of you! What's the occasion you're buying for?"

You: "We've had a stressful couple weeks with my mother's visit, and I want to really thank her for making it all work."

Florist: "Such a great idea. Do you think she would prefer fresh flowers or a plant of some type?"

You: "Definitely fresh flowers today. And I do know she loves pink, and she hates those lily flowers."

Florist: "Well then, let's look in our display cooler and select something we think she'll like."

You: "There's so much to choose from. Why don't you make something you think she'd like, say, in about the $50.00 range. And can you deliver that for me this afternoon? She won't be home till after 2".

Florist: "We'd be happy to do that for you. Let's go back over to the counter and I'll get some information about the delivery".

That's just how the sale should go, nice and easy. You've given some information, been asked about some information, and you've let the florist do their job. No looking endlessly through a catalogue of confusing pictures, taking up everyone's time because you think you need to be the one to decide on the flowers to send. Yes, it's great if you know how to do that, but let's be real: how many guys really know the difference? We don't like to be told how to do OUR job, right?

So put the power in the place it should be. Doing that is sure to make the whole experience fun and rewarding. And as long as the person at the other end loves what you've sent, everyone's done a great job. You can still be the macho hombre we all know you are, ready to take those sexual rewards that I'm sure are close at hand.

Money Will Feed The Beast

It sucks big time, but economies play a key role in the retail prices of things we buy. When dollars are everywhere, things are usually higher in price and we don't mind because the money flow is there. When the financial picture ain't so sunny, that flow either stops completely or is a bit more tamed. This has happened for centuries, and no matter how fiscally responsible our country is (who am I trying to kid!), I think it will continue for years to come. The 21st century is definitely proving that fact again.

With that in mind, the prices of retail flowers fluctuate according to how the economy is rolling, but it all depends on what you're asking for in the design of your bouquet. Simple designs (tasteful, but with less higher priced flowers) will always have simple prices, while more extravagance (larger in flower quantity with more expensive flowers such as orchids, roses, hydrangea, tropical varieties) necessitates digging deeper in that wallet. You may get some better deals when our dollar isn't worth so much but you're still going to pay what you're going to pay. It's an occasion you're usually buying for so it might be only once or twice a year that you'll do this (plus all the small bouquets you pick up to keep your love alive!). It'd be great if you'd send flowers monthly, but I'm realistic about what to expect from most clients.

Most florists are competitively priced and if someone is charging more for a design, they generally do more (especially creatively) than the other guy. But getting a relationship established with a local florist is a key way to get extreme value both economically and visually. That's a real plus if you want to make that hottie want you too. Use that florist exclusively (after they've proven themselves to you) and it really makes the whole process flow. That florist will really want to wow your loved one each time by creating different designs. Everyone wins in this scenario. Now back to the dinero part. In my shop, we started designing things at $10.00. Sounds great, right? But it's a lower end single flower like a carnation in a "less expensive" (cheap!) bud vase, and not delivered. But for the right situation it's great. More stems in the same vase run $15.00, $17.50, $20.00, $22.50. Same vase, just different types of flowers and/or more of them. Most daily arrangements run $35.00 on up, with most clients spending an average of $40.00 to $75.00. Although you can spend as high an amount as you want, the designs at any price are nice. It's just that the more you spend, the more you get. I have a client who was sending designs weekly to a new lady he wanted to really impress. I worked with him, suggesting to start slow (had to hold him back a bit) then building up that floral momentum and size if everything went well. It began in the $22.50 range that went up to $100.00 as the weeks went on. Our floral designs got him right where he wanted, and there were romantic weekends spent together just after the first month. This is a prime example of what this book is all about and, again, the value you can really create with great floral knowledge.

You've got to spend what your budget can bear but don't be a cheap ass. Spend at least 50 bucks to make some impression, but at least double that or more to really get someone's attention. And if your budget is tight do the small vase thing and drop it by yourself. It's the thought that really counts, and this particular "counting" goes a long way for future rewards. And please don't be one of those whiners bitching about the price of flowers. Guys will say "flowers are expensive!" but then spend bucks on a TV sports game or a case of beer (ok, sometimes beer's a priority). But you have to realize that the value of feelings you create with sending flowers far outweighs the money you'll ever spend. Get this embedded in your brain to make sure your sexual gratification path is on its way. And truly allow yourself to enjoy that ride!

And This Ass-Bite Has More To Say?!

If I've learned anything in my 40+ years in the floral industry, it's that the customer is king. But just because the customer is king does not mean that they have all the tools to do the right thing when it comes to flower buying. That's when we experienced florists come in to save the day, and become those heroes that make you studs the ultimate heroes. Our trusted knowledge is something to take advantage of, and that knowledge is sure to get you your most sought after reward: testosterone driven sex that will be repeated over and over again just as long as you continue to buy flowers!

Now, I can't totally guarantee that buying flowers will get you laid. YOU have to do some leg work, be smart, and charismatic. Show your stuff, be an hombre that's not overbearing, and let them know you really care. Then when you add those beautiful floral bouquets to the equation, you'll find that the journey will go a heck of a lot better to get you those rewards you so desperately want and deserve. That much I can guarantee!

The Authentic Flower Guy: Mutation Of The Finest

The knowledgeable stud that wrote this book has been in the floral industry for over 40 years, beginning that journey as a delivery driver learning flower preparation and other valuable facets of the industry. After a few years as delivery driver, Joe moved to Carpinteria, Ca. and became a laborer at Sandyland Nursery. This nursery was one of the largest in California and one of the first (if not the first) growing nurseries to sell to the chain stores, mainly Safeway at the time. Gaining valuable experience in the science of growing foliage plants, he worked his way up that great ladder to become an assistant grower. This was achieved without any formal college training in the horticulture field, so is quite a feather in this guy's cap. From there, Joe got married to his high school sweetheart, Dawn, and then moved back to his home town, Santa Maria, Ca. to work at another wholesale growing nursery as grower/manager.

After 5 years of being in the growing part of the industry, the allure of floral design progressed into the purchase of their flower shop, Camfeldt's Flowers, where Joe continued his floral journey. During the 32 years of owning this retail shop, Joe became a member of AIFD (The American Institute of Floral Designers) the premier association for a floral designer to belong to. From this Joe designed for the California State Floral Association, and continues mentoring the Cal Poly San Luis Obispo AIFD student chapter. His current passion is sharing his experiences and being a "floral concierge" to clients and the floral industry through his business JP Designs. His mantra "educate, motivate, and create!" represents the passion he shares in the floral world. And yes, he uses the tools taught in this book to maintain his sexual journey to last a lifetime!

Sources:

1. Joe Guggia's floral experienced journey

2. Information Article, Testosterone, Encyclopedia Wikipedia

3. The Tradition of Giving Flowers, Victor Epand, Ezine Articles

4. Where Did The Tradition Of Giving Flowers Start?, Mark Scott, XZcution-Articles Directory